Unsolved!

THE MYSTERY OF THE GHOSTS OF FLIGHT 401

Kathryn Walker

based on original text by Brian Innes

Crabtree Publishing Company

www.crabtreebooks.com

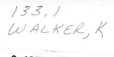

Crabtree Publishing Company

www.crabtreebooks.com

Author: Kathryn Walker
    based on original text by Brian Innes
Project editor: Kathryn Walker
Picture researcher: Rachel Tisdale
Managing editor: Miranda Smith
Art director: Jeni Child
Design manager: David Poole
Editorial director: Lindsey Lowe
Children's publisher: Anne O'Daly
Editor: Molly Aloian
Proofreaders: Adrianna Morganelli, Crystal Sikkens
Project coordinator: Robert Walker
Production coordinator: Katherine Kantor
Prepress technician: Katherine Kantor

This edition published in 2009 by
Crabtree Publishing Inc.

The Brown Reference Group plc
First Floor
9-17 St. Albans Place
London N1 0NX
www.brownreference.com

Copyright © 2008 The Brown Reference Group plc

Photographs:
Airliners.net: Ellis M. Chernoff: p. 14–15 (center);
    Sam Chui: p. 6–7; Scott Kiel: p. 19
www.aviationpictures.com: Austin J. Brown LBIPP:
    p. 4–5, 18, 20, 22–23
Corbis: p. 12–13, 15 (top), 16, 21
Fortean Picture Library: p. 27
Getty Images: Ted Russell: p. 28–29
Historical Museum of Southern Florida: p. 10, 11
Istockphoto: p. 30; John Sfondilias: p. 26
George Lainhart: p. 25
Shutterstock: Angelo Garibaldi: p. 24; Slowfish: p. 9;
    Peter Sobolev: p. 17; Stephen Strathdee: cover;
    Stephen Sweet: p. 8

Every effort has been made to trace the
owners of copyrighted material.

Library and Archives Canada Cataloguing in Publication

Walker, Kathryn, 1957-
    The mystery of the ghosts of Flight 401 / Kathryn Walker ;
based on original text by Brian Innes.

(Unsolved!)
Includes index.
ISBN 978-0-7787-4142-8 (bound).--ISBN 978-0-7787-4155-8 (pbk.)

    1. Ghosts--Juvenile literature. 2. Aircraft accidents-- Miscellanea--
Juvenile literature. I. Innes, Brian II. Title. III. Series: Unsolved!
(St. Catharines, Ont.)

BF1461.W34 2008   j133.1'2975939   C2008-904326-X

Library of Congress Cataloging-in-Publication Data

Walker, Kathryn.
    The mystery of the ghosts of Flight 401 / Kathryn Walker ; based on original text by
Brian Innes.
        p. cm. -- (Unsolved!)
    Includes index.
    ISBN-13: 978-0-7787-4155-8 (pbk. : alk. paper)
    ISBN-10: 0-7787-4155-9 (pbk. : alk. paper)
    ISBN-13: 978-0-7787-4142-8 (reinforced library binding : alk. paper)
    ISBN-10: 0-7787-4142-7 (reinforced library binding : alk. paper)
    1. Ghosts--Juvenile literature. 2. Aircraft accidents--Miscellanea--Juvenile literature.
I. Innes, Brian. II. Title.
    BF1461.W34 2009
    133.1'2975939--dc22

        2008030109

Crabtree Publishing Company

Published in Canada
Crabtree Publishing
616 Welland Ave.
St. Catharines, ON
L2M 5V6

Published in the United States
Crabtree Publishing
PMB16A
350 Fifth Ave., Suite 3308
New York, NY 10118

Contents

The Fatal Flight

...In 1972, a flight to Miami ended in disaster.

At 9:29 P.M. on December 29, 1972, Eastern Airlines plane number 310 took off from Kennedy International Airport (JFK), New York. The plane was on a nonstop run to Miami, Florida. This run was known as Flight 401.

Number 310 was one of twelve new Eastern Airlines planes. These were Lockheed L-1011 TriStars. Each plane could carry more than 250 passengers.

At about 11:30 P.M., the pilots began to prepare to land. But by 11:42 P.M. the plane was losing height fast over the Florida **Everglades**. A few seconds later, it crashed into the dark **swampland**.

There was a burst of orange flame and a cloud of black smoke. At first there was silence. Then came the cries and screams of the injured.

>> **Everglades** — A region in southern Florida

How Strange...

◎ The flight crew did not realize the plane was losing height until seconds before the crash.

◎ Plane #310 had been flying for just over four months.

"Number 310 was one of twelve new Eastern Airlines planes."

EASTERN

This is an Eastern Airlines L-1011 TriStar. On December 29, 1972, a plane like this one crashed into the Florida Everglades.

What Went Wrong?

...In the darkness, no one noticed that the ground was getting closer.

Eastern Airlines was very proud of its new EL-1011 TriStars. The airline described the TriStar as "the quietest, cleanest plane in the skies." They nicknamed the new planes "Whisperliners."

On December 29, 1972, TriStar #310 had 163 passengers onboard. It also had a **crew** of 13 people. Captain Bob Loft, Copilot Bert Stockstill, and Flight Engineer Don Repo were in the **cockpit**. The men had flown many times.

Every modern plane is fitted with a "black box" flight recorder. This device records important information about a flight. After a crash, investigators look for the black box. It helps them to discover why the crash happened.

The flight recorder from TriStar #310 was found in the wreckage. It soon explained what had gone wrong.

>> **crew** — The people who work onboard an aircraft or ship

"The airline described the TriStar as 'the quietest, cleanest plane in the skies.'"

This is the flight crew of a TriStar L-1011. Inside the cockpit, there are thousands of lights, dials, and switches.

>> **cockpit** — The area at the front of an aircraft, from which the pilots control the plane

At about 11:30 P.M., TriStar #310 was nearing Miami International Airport. Bob Loft told Bert Stockstill to lower the landing gear. These are the wheels that allow a plane to land safely.

A Light Bulb Problem

Captain Loft noticed that one of the lights on his control panel was not lit. If the landing wheel at the front of the plane had come down, this light should have come on. The crew thought the wheel probably had come down. They thought that the light bulb might be faulty. But they had to be sure.

The plane circled while the crew tried to sort out the problem. They tried to replace the light bulb, but it would not come out. Don Repo went into a **compartment** under the cockpit. He went to see if the wheels were down.

As the plane circled over the Everglades, the crew switched to autopilot. Autopilot is a device that steers a plane along its course without help from a person. It should have kept the plane circling at the same height.

"The plane circled while the crew tried to sort out the problem."

FLIGHT RECORDER
DO NOT OPEN

This is what a black box flight recorder looks like. As you can see, it is actually bright orange. This makes it easier to find after a crash.

>> **compartment** — A separate area or section

This is a photo of the marshy Everglades. By day, it is easy to lose your way. At night, it is almost impossible to know where you are.

An Accidental Bump

It seems as if Captain Loft leaned over to help with the light bulb. In doing this, he accidentally bumped the steering column. A steering column is like the steering wheel of a car. Pressing on the steering column turned off the autopilot. The plane began to drop toward the swamps.

The men did not realize that the autopilot was switched off. As the plane lost height, there should have been warning **chimes**. But all three were busy. They did not notice the chimes.

Outside, everything was black. Nobody saw that the ground was getting closer.

How Strange...

- After the crash, investigators found that TriStar #310's landing wheels had come down.

- A faulty light bulb had caused a problem that led to the crash.

>> **chime** — A tone, similar to the sound made by a bell or clock

This is the wreckage of TriStar #310. It lies scattered over a large area of the swampland.

The plane was traveling at 250 miles (402 kilometers) per hour when it hit the ground. It broke up as it moved through the mud and grass. Passengers were flung into the water. Some were still strapped to their seats.

The Rescue

That night, Robert Marquis was fishing for frogs in the Everglades. The TriStar passed low over him. Then he saw an explosion. Marquis headed toward the crash scene in his **airboat**. As soon as he got there, he began dragging injured people out of the water.

"Passengers were flung into the water. Some were still strapped to their seats."

>> **airboat** — A boat driven by an aircraft propeller that can be used in swamps

At 12:15 A.M., two rescue helicopters arrived. They spotted the light of Marquis' airboat in the swamps. The darkness and the mud made rescue very difficult. It was hard for rescue vehicles to reach the crash site. They had to drive along a narrow **levee**.

There had been 176 people on board TriStar #310. Only 75 people survived. Captain Bob Loft and Bert Stockstill died in the plane. Don Repo died of his injuries in the hospital.

This photograph was taken during the rescue operation in 1972. A child that survived the crash is being taken to the hospital.

How Strange...

- A two-month-old baby survived the crash. She had been seated on her mother's lap.

- A poodle was found alive at the scene of the crash. It had been traveling under a passenger's seat.

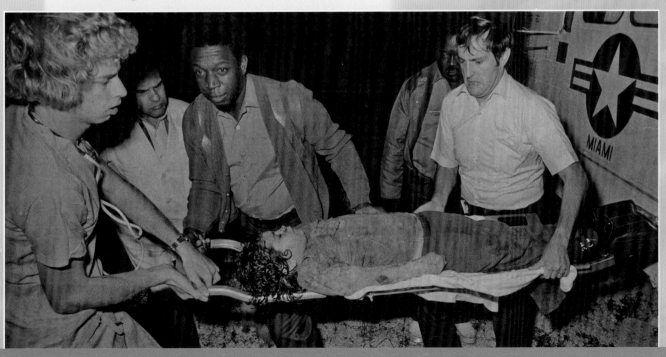

A Narrow Escape

...One person seemed to know that a plane was going to crash.

Two weeks before the crash, an Eastern Airlines **flight attendant** had an upsetting experience. She imagined that a plane crash was going to happen. In her mind, she saw the plane crash in the Everglades.

The flight attendant told her **coworkers** what she had seen. They asked her if they would be onboard that plane. "No," she answered. "But it's going to be real close."

On December 29, the flight attendant and her coworkers were on TriStar #310 when it arrived at JFK Airport. They were told to take the plane on to Miami. At the last minute, there was a change of plan. Another crew replaced them on the fatal Flight 401.

How Strange...

The flight attendant told her coworkers the crash would happen close to the New Year.

The woman had experienced similar feelings before. The things she saw had come true.

>> **flight attendant** — A person who looks after passengers on an airplane

This is the passenger cabin aboard a TriStar L-1011. One of the flight attendants is handing out magazines.

The Pilots Reappear

...After the Flight 401 crash, strange things began to happen.

In the months after the crash, crew members on other TriStar L-1011s reported some unusual events. Many of these took place aboard TriStar #318.

Like other L-1011s, plane #318 had a **galley**. At first, flight attendants reported feeling very cold there. But the **thermometer** showed that the temperature was normal. Then, one day, a flight attendant in the galley suddenly noticed a white cloud.

As the flight attendant watched, a face appeared in the cloud. She saw it quite clearly. She said it was the face of Don Repo. He had been the flight engineer onboard the crashed TriStar #310.

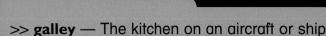

Captain Bob Loft is pictured top left. To his right is Flight Engineer Don Repo. Both men died as a result of the Flight 401 crash. Many people said they saw the dead men onboard other TriStars.

"As the flight attendant watched, a face appeared in the cloud."

A month or so later, something even more startling happened aboard TriStar #318.

An Extra Passenger

The plane was at Newark Airport, ready to take off. A flight attendant checked the number of passengers. There was one too many.

The attendant found the extra passenger sitting in **first class**. He was wearing an Eastern Airlines captain's uniform and staring ahead.

This is Newark airport. In 1973, TriStar #318 was delayed here while crew members searched for the extra passenger.

>> **first class** — The area on an aircraft with the best seats and service

The flight attendant spoke to the man, but he did not respond. Other passengers watched with interest. Then the pilot came over to speak to the man. He stopped in his tracks. "It's Bob Loft!" he whispered. Loft had been captain of the crashed TriStar #310.

Then something amazing happened. The man vanished in front of everybody. The crew searched the plane from end to end. There was no sign of the extra passenger.

"...the pilot... stopped in his tracks. 'It's Bob Loft!' he whispered."

Mysterious Mist
Another time, a passenger spotted a glowing mist over the right **wingtip**. He pointed this out to a flight attendant.

Whenever the mist settled on the wing, the plane rolled to the right. The flight attendant watched for a minute or two. Then she called the flight engineer. He said it was a cloud, but even he was puzzled by its strange behavior.

A view of a plane wing seen through a passenger window. In 1973, a passenger on TriStar #318 saw something strange over the plane's right wingtip.

>> **wingtip** — The extreme outer edge of an aircraft wing

In February 1974, another strange event was reported on TriStar #318. It happened during a flight to Mexico City and Acapulco.

A Ghostly Face

A flight attendant was preparing food in the galley. She clearly saw the face of Don Repo. It was reflected in the glass of an oven door.

Another flight attendant joined her in the galley. She could see the man's face, too. The two women also called the flight engineer to the galley. As he looked at the oven, the face of Don Repo spoke to him. "Watch out for fire on this plane," it said.

The plane arrived safely in Mexico City. But then there was a problem with one of the engines. The last stage of the flight was **canceled**.

"She clearly saw the face of Don Repo. It was reflected in the glass of an oven door."

This Tristar L-1011 is being prepared for flight. During 1973 and 1974, there were many unexplained events on board TriStars.

>> **canceled** — Stopped from going ahead as planned

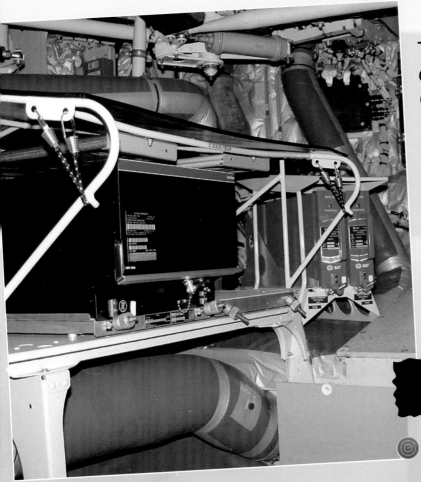

This is the small compartment under the cockpit of an aircraft. Crew sometimes call this the "hell hole." It was where Don Repo was at the time TriStar #310 crashed.

Strange Knocking

On a flight to Miami, a crew member heard a loud knocking. It was coming from the compartment below the cockpit. The man opened a trapdoor in the floor. He shone a light into the compartment. There was nobody down there. Then the crew member turned to look at the **control panel**. At that moment, he saw a face he knew well. It was Don Repo.

How Strange...

A group of workers bringing food aboard TriStar #318 left in fear. They said they had seen a flight engineer vanish in the galley.

On another TriStar, an upset passenger was taken away on a stretcher. She had seen the man next to her disappear.

Before a plane takes off, it has to be checked over. Equipment is checked to make sure it is working properly. These are called preflight checks. Some pilots claimed they saw Don Repo in the cockpit when they were doing their **preflight checks**.

Watching Over

On one occasion, a flight engineer entered the cockpit to make his checks. He found a man in an Eastern Airlines uniform sitting at his place. The flight engineer recognized the man as Don Repo.

"Don't worry about your preflight check," Repo told him. "I've already done it." Then the figure vanished.

Afterward, a captain on another flight said he had seen Don Repo, too. "There will never be another crash of a L-1011. We won't let it happen," Repo had said. It was as if Loft and Repo were watching over the aircraft.

This is the engineer's control panel in the cockpit of a TriStar. It is where Don Repo would have sat onboard TriStar #310.

>> **preflight check** — A check carried out on an aircraft before it takes off

Reused Parts

Undamaged parts from old or crashed planes are sometimes saved and reused. This is known as salvage. Parts of the crashed Flight 401 plane were salvaged. They were built into other TriStar L-1011s.

Most of the ghostly appearances were reported on planes that contained parts of the crashed TriStar. Could the salvaged parts have brought ghosts with them?

This photograph of TriStar #310 was taken the day after the crash. Eastern Airlines were able to save and reuse many parts of the plane.

How Strange...

- A flight attendant claimed she saw the face of Bob Loft when she looked inside an **overhead locker**.

- An oven from the crashed plane was put into TriStar #318. It was in this oven that some crew members saw Don Repo's face.

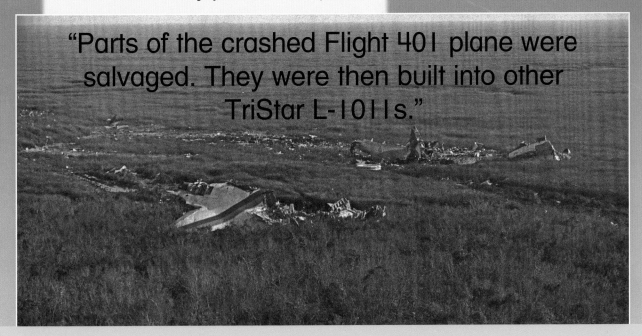

"Parts of the crashed Flight 401 plane were salvaged. They were then built into other TriStar L-1011s."

John Fuller Investigates

...John G. Fuller heard **rumors** about the ghosts of flight 401.

John G. Fuller was a **journalist**. In 1974, he decided to find out all about these ghostly events. He spoke to many crew members about the strange things they had seen.

Fuller learned more about how parts from the crashed TriStar had been built into other planes. He also discovered that all these reused parts were now being removed. This included some parts that had nothing wrong with them.

Eastern Airlines said they knew nothing about any ghosts on their planes. But why had the airline ordered the removal of all parts from the Flight 401 crash? Perhaps they hoped to get rid of the ghosts this way. Or maybe they were trying to stop the rumors from spreading.

>> **rumor** — Something that a lot of people are saying, but that might not be true

"Eastern Airlines said they knew nothing about any ghosts on their planes."

A TriStar L-1011 gets ready to take off. For months after the crash of Flight 401, there were many unexplained events aboard these planes.

John Fuller got in touch with Eastern Airlines pilots Rich Craig and Stan Chambers. They were interested in things related to the mind and spirit.

Some people believe that the spirit is part of a person that cannot be seen. These people think that the spirit can go on living after the body dies.

Contacting Don Repo

Fuller met with the two pilots and their wives. Together, they tried to get in touch with the spirit of Don Repo. None of them had ever met Repo.

After some minutes, Stan Chambers spoke. He said that he had a clear picture in his mind of a man. The man was wearing a uniform. His hair was dark with some gray. He had **sideburns**. The person he described sounded like Don Repo.

"...they tried to get in touch with the spirit of Don Repo."

This is a view of the Florida Everglades. On the night of December 29, 1972, it became a scene of horror when Flight 401 crashed into its **marshy** ground.

>> **sideburns** — Hair growing down the sides of a man's face

Feeling Fear

Stan Chambers said the man was saying something about a trapdoor. Chambers said "He's trapped down in this hole and he can't get up." Mrs. Craig seemed to be sharing Repo's feelings. She felt pain in her head. She also felt water rushing into the plane and great fear.

Everyone at the meeting believed they had been in touch with Don Repo. They thought that his ghostly appearances had been attempts to get in touch with aircraft crew.

This is Robert Marquis in his airboat. In 1972, Marquis rescued many people from the Flight 401 crash. This picture was taken in 2007, when survivors gathered at the crash site to remember the dead.

>> **marshy** — Land that is flooded in wet seasons or at high tide

"...her husband used to collect Indian-head pennies."

During his **investigations**, John Fuller met a flight attendant named Elizabeth Manzione. Manzione joined him in his investigations.

Messages from the Dead

Together, Fuller and Manzione carried out some experiments. They tried to get in touch with the spirits of people who had died in the Flight 401 crash.

During one experiment, Fuller and Manzione received messages from Don Repo. The messages were for Repo's wife and daughter. But they did not make much sense.

This is the front (left) and back (right) of an Indian-head coin. Don Repo had collected Indian-head pennies similar to this.

>> **investigation** — The process of trying to find out all the facts

One of the messages was "Did mice leave that family closet?" Another was "To go into wastebasket…pennies sit there…boy's room."

Fuller and Manzione met with Don Repo's wife and daughter. Mrs. Repo was startled when she heard the messages. She understood what they meant.

Mrs Repo said that there had been mice in the attic above their closet. Also, her husband used to collect Indian-head pennies. There was a small barrel full of them in her son's room.

The Hauntings Stop

Soon afterward, people stopped seeing Loft and Repo on board the TriStars. It was as if their spirits were finally at rest. John Fuller went on to write about the story in a book. He named the book The Ghost of Flight 401.

This book by John Fuller appeared in 1976. It sold many copies and was later turned into a television movie.

0-425-03553-0 • $2.25 • A BERKLEY MEDALLION BOOK

THE REAL-LIFE SUPERNATURAL INCIDENT THAT GROUNDED A JUMBO JET

JOHN G. FULLER

THE GHOST OF FLIGHT 401

Was It Real?

...Did people actually see the ghosts of Flight 401? Or did they just imagine them?

Some people feel sure that people's spirits live on after their bodies die. Others also believe that these spirits sometimes appear to living people.

When a person dies suddenly, he or she may leave many things unfinished. Some people think this can cause the spirit great worry and upset.

The spirit may then appear as a ghost. It needs to make sure that all is well with the ones it has left behind. Only then can the spirit rest in peace.

Could this explain why people saw the ghosts of Bob Loft and Don Repo? The men had died unexpectedly. Maybe their ghosts were trying to keep people safe on other TriStar L-101Is.

How Strange...

During a flight of plane #318, a man's voice came over the **loudspeaker**. He told people to fasten their seat belts and to follow the usual safety **precautions**. But none of the crew had made the announcement!

>> **loudspeaker** — A system for making announcements heard in public areas

"Maybe (their) ghosts were trying to keep people safe on other TriStar L-1011s."

During 1973 and 1974, many pilots claimed they had seen Don Repo. He often appeared when they were doing their preflight checks.

Many people enjoy ghost stories and creepy feelings. People may have imagined or lied about the ghosts of Flight 401. But some of the ghostly occurences were seen by several people. It is hard to believe that everyone was mistaken or telling lies.

Could it be that these people had been expecting or hoping to see a ghost? This may have made them more ready to believe that they did see something. Once one person says they have seen a ghost, others often think they have seen one, too.

Special Energy?

Some people wonder if the strong feelings of a dying person can produce a special energy. What if surroundings can trap that energy in some way? Then images of the dead people might appear again and again, like a recording.

We do not know if these people really did see the ghosts of Flight 401. There have been many explanations for ghosts and hauntings. But we have no scientific proof that they really happen.

Many people have reported seeing ghostly figures. Some say that they have received messages from the dead.

>> **energy** — Force or power to do things

Glossary

airboat A boat driven by an aircraft propeller that can be used in swamps

canceled Stopped from going ahead as planned

chime A tone, similar to the sound made by a bell or clock

cockpit The area at the front of an aircraft, from which the pilots control the plane

compartment A separate area or section

control panel A panel or board with switches, dials, and instruments for operating equipment

coworker Someone who works with another in the same company

crew The people who work onboard an aircraft or ship

energy Force or power to do things

Everglades A region in southern Florida

first class The area on an aircraft with the best seats and service

flight attendant A person who looks after passengers on an airplane

galley The kitchen on an aircraft or ship

haunting The repeated appearance of a ghost in a particular place

investigation The process of trying to find out all the facts

journalist Someone who writes or reports news, particularly for newspapers

levee An embankment or raised area, built to prevent flooding

loudspeaker A system for making announcements heard in public areas

marshy Land that is flooded in wet seasons or at high tide

overhead locker A storage area located above the passengers' heads in an aircraft

precaution An action taken to protect against possible danger

preflight check A check carried out on an aircraft before it takes off

rumor Something that a lot of people are saying, but that might not be true

sideburns Hair growing down the sides of a man's face

swampland An area of wet ground or marsh

thermometer An instrument for measuring temperature

wingtip The extreme outer edge of an aircraft wing

Index

Further Reading

• Cohen, David and Susan. Hauntings and Horrors: The Ultimate
  Guide to Spooky America. Dutton Juvenile, 2002.
• Donkin, Andrew. Spooky Spinechiller, "DK Readers (Level 4:
  Proficient Readers)" series. DK Children, 2000.
• Summers, Lori. The Ghost Hunter's Handbook, "Field Guides to
  the Paranormal" series. Price Stern Sloan, 2002.
• Woods, Mary B. and Michael. Air Disasters, "Disasters Up Close"
  series. Lerner Publications, 2007.

Printed in the U.S.A.